dairy cookbook

Notes

Standard level spoon measurements are used in all recipes.
1 tablespoon = one 15 ml spoon
1 teaspoon = one 5 ml spoon

Both imperial and metric measurements have been given in all recipes. Use one set of measurements only and not a mixture of both.

Eggs should be medium unless otherwise stated. The Department of Health advises that eggs should not be consumed raw. This book contains dishes made with raw or lightly cooked eggs. It is prudent for more vulnerable people such as pregnant and nursing mothers, invalids, the elderly, babies and young children to avoid uncooked or lightly cooked dishes made with eggs. Once prepared, these dishes should be kept refrigerated and used promptly.

Milk should be full fat unless otherwise stated.

Fresh herbs should be used unless otherwise stated. If unavailable, use dried herbs as an alternative but halve the quantities stated. Ovens should be pre-heated to the specified temperature – if using a fan-assisted oven, follow manufacturer's instructions for adjusting the time and the temperature.

All microwave information is based on a 650 watt oven. Follow manufacturer's instructions for an oven with a different wattage.

Pepper should be freshly ground black pepper unless otherwise stated.

Nuts and nut derivatives
This book includes dishes made with nuts and nut derivatives. It is advisable for readers with known allergic reactions to nuts and nut derivatives and those who may be potentially vulnerable to these allergies, such as pregnant and nursing mothers, invalids, the elderly, babies and children, to avoid dishes made with nuts and nut oils. It is also prudent to check the labels of pre-prepared ingredients for the possible inclusion of nut derivatives.

Vegetarians
Vegetarians should look for the 'V' symbol on a cheese to ensure it is made with vegetarian rennet. There are vegetarian forms of Parmesan, Feta, Cheddar, Cheshire, Red Leicester, dolcelatte and many goats' cheeses, among others.

Laurence and Gilles Laurendon

dairy cookbook

Photographs by Akiko Ida and Pierre Javelle

HACHETTE Illustrated

Milk

Farm milk straight from the cow is by far the best, but you have to appreciate its very strong herby flavour! In the shops, the most readily available fresh milk is the pasteurized variety, which tastes good and is ideal for cooking and cake making.
UHT milk, which has been sterilized at 150°C (300°F), is convenient because it can be stored easily.
Powdered milk may not appeal, but it takes up very little room in the store cupboard and is really easy to use.
Condensed milk can be consumed for pleasure but, whether sweetened or unsweetened, it is also useful for cooking and cake baking. Of course, from the calorie point of view, it's not the best kind!
Milk may be full fat, semi-skimmed or skimmed, but full fat is used in these recipes.

Butter

Butter is good just as it is, spread on a slice of bread, but it also makes the dishes you prepare smooth and creamy.
Sample the various butters made in the UK and elsewhere in Europe, and you will find a variety of tastes, both the usual salted and the more delicate unsalted. The extra fine label on good quality butter is a guarantee that it has been made without any frozen cream. Its flavour is truly superfine!

Cream

Pasteurized or raw, it is crème fraîche that has the finest flavour. With its thick texture, it is the perfect accompaniment to fresh fruit, tarts or gateaux.
Whipping cream is less rich and calorie-loaded than double cream. It whips up quickly if it is chilled first and can be used to make plain whipped, or Chantilly, cream in an instant.
UHT sterilized cream keeps very well for a few weeks. Have it in reserve in the store cupboard, as it is very convenient to use!

Fromage blanc

This is simply a curd with a sharp delicate flavour, that has been strained to produce a slightly granular soft white cheese, or else a cheese that has been whisked to give it a smooth, creamier-tasting consistency.

Petits-suisses

A speciality of Normandy, these mouthwatering little desserts combine fromage blanc and crème fraîche. And they're oh! so creamy!

Yogurt

This thin fermented milk, mild but with a slightly acidic taste, is eaten in many parts of the world: by the Tibetans, by the Mongols of Central Asia, in India, Turkey, Greece …
Yogurt is available in the shops in various forms and textures. These will depend on whether it has been made with full-fat, semi-skimmed or skimmed milk; cow's milk or goat's milk. Greek yogurt is the name given to a thick, creamy, high-fat yogurt originating from Greece

Ribot milk

This fermented milk is a very old Breton country recipe. Served as a drink with buckwheat pancakes, it is a feast stuffed full of vitamins! It would be worth trying to track down some on your next trip to France.

Mascarpone

This especially creamy fromage frais from Italy is made with cream from cows' milk, and is ideal for desserts.

Cream cheese

A cheese from the UK also made with cream. It has a very creamy flavour with just a hint of acidity.

Ricotta

An Italian cheese made from whey that has been re-cooked (ri-cotta), and is collected after the milk has been heated to make a fromage blanc. Delicious in pasta dishes!

Home-made butter

Home-made yogurt

Home-made fromage frais

Home-made butter

Makes 175 g (6 oz) unsalted butter
Preparation time: 12 minutes

1 glass jar with lid
(jam jar or preserving jar)

400 ml (14 fl oz) thick crème fraîche

Pour the crème fraîche into the jar, screw on the
lid and shake it for about 12 minutes.
The butter should form gradually. Put it through
a sieve to extract the water, then replace the
butter in the jar, cover it with cold water and
start to shake it again. Rinse again, shaking it
another 2 or 3 times, until the rinsing water
runs quite clear. Drain and put in a cool place,
or the refrigerator.
Tip: Use a good quality crème fraîche. Take it
out of the refrigerator in advance so that it is
at room temperature. However, the jar should
be very cold.

Home-made yogurt
You can make home-made yogurt without
a yogurt-maker.

Makes 8 yogurts
Preparation time: 10 minutes
Cooking time: 5 minutes
Standing time: overnight

1 casserole dish
1 food thermometer (optional)
8 small glass yogurt pots

1 litre (1¾ pints) fresh milk
1 small natural 'live' yogurt

Pour water into the casserole dish until it comes
half-way up, then bring to the boil. Pour the
water away and cover the casserole to preserve
the heat.
Heat the milk in a large saucepan until it reaches
52°C (125°F).
Remove from the ring immediately and mix the
yogurt into the hot milk. Stir well, fill the pots
with it, and arrange them in the casserole.
Cover and leave to stand overnight.

Home-made fromage frais

Serves 4
Preparation time: 5 minutes
Cooking time: 5 minutes

500 ml (17 fl oz) fresh milk
4 tablespoons lemon juice
freshly ground salt and pepper

Heat the milk in a saucepan until it reaches 40°C
(104°F). Pour the lemon juice into the hot milk
and stir.
Specks of white curd will form immediately. Pour
it through a fine sieve and put the curds into a
bowl. Mix well, add salt and pepper, and enjoy
the fromage frais on a slice of bread.

home comforts

Those memories of home, when mother used to surprise us with her milk shakes the pale colour of dreams. Oh, those mouthwatering milk shakes, sweet-tasting dumplings and gorgeous gratins! Go on, eat up, you need strength for school work!

The soup, full of flavour, she would insist was good for us? All right, we'll eat it just to please her! But really, we adored it!

And then the home-made caramels we slipped in our pockets, which lingered long in the mouth so that we could have a competition to see whose piece lasted the longest!

Little cream pots

Serves 4
Preparation time: 10 minutes
Cooking time: 30 minutes

4–6 small, round porcelain pots with tall sides

400 ml (14 fl oz) milk
100 ml (3½ fl oz) crème fraîche
2 teaspoons dried verbena leaves
6 egg yolks
40 g (1½ oz) caster sugar

Preheat the oven to 150°C (300°F), Gas Mark 2.
Gently heat the milk and crème fraîche together
in a saucepan then remove from the heat, add
the verbena leaves and cover. Leave to infuse for
10 minutes.
Remove the verbena leaves from the pan.
Put the egg yolks and caster sugar in a large
bowl and whisk until the mixture becomes pale.
Add the milk and crème fraîche while continuing
to mix.
Fill the pots with this mixture. Put them in a
high-sided dish, like a roasting tin or a cast iron
casserole.
Pour warm water into the dish until it comes
halfway up the cream pots.
Place in the oven for about 20 minutes.
Leave to cool before eating.

Caramels made with milk and butter

Makes about 12 caramels
Preparation time: 5 minutes
Cooking time: 20 minutes

1 metal ice-tray

sunflower oil
200 ml (7 fl oz) milk
175 g (6 oz) caster sugar
30 g (1¼ oz) butter
2 tablespoons honey

Carefully oil the bottom and sides of the ice-tray.
Pour the milk into a heavy-based saucepan and
add the caster sugar, butter and honey. Bring it
to simmering point and allow it to cook over a
low heat for about 20 minutes, stirring regularly
with a spoon.
The mixture will gradually thicken and take on
a beautiful caramel colour.
Pour into the ice-tray while still hot and leave to
cool to room temperature. Cut into 12 caramels
with a knife.
Depending on the cooking time, you will have
either extra soft caramels (the best ones, with
their amazing flavour of honey and butter,
although they are not always very presentable),
soft caramels or really hard ones, which can be
sucked for a long time.

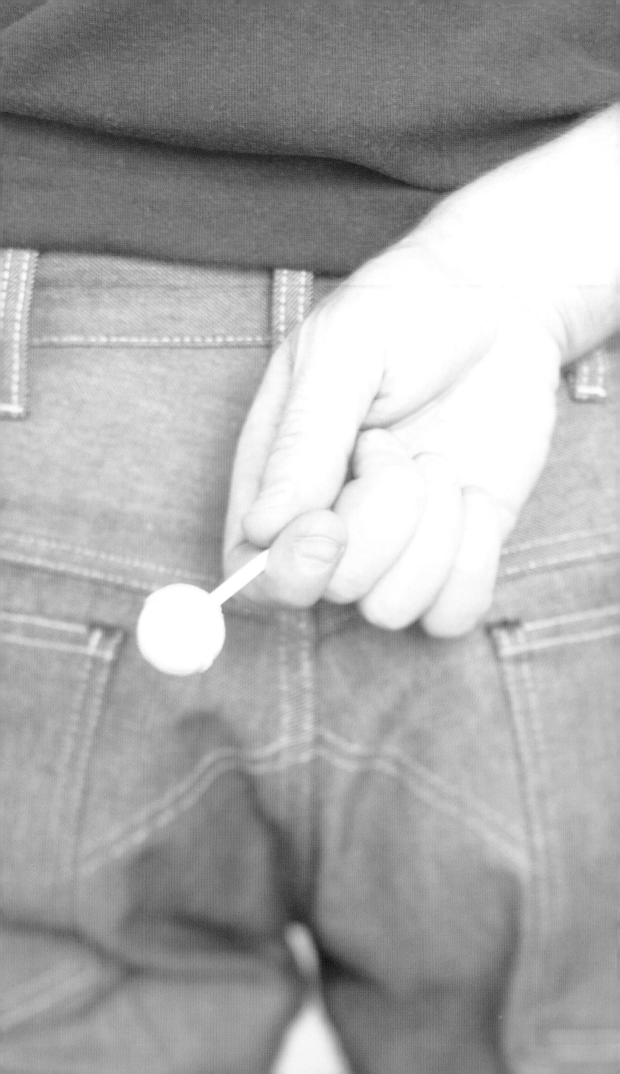

Very simple rice pudding

Very simple rice pudding

Serve 4
Preparation time: 5 minutes
Cooking time: 35 minutes

1 serving dish

1 vanilla pod
200 g (7 oz) round grain (pudding) rice
1 litre (1¾ pints) milk
125 g (4 oz) caster sugar

Cut the vanilla pod in half lengthways with the point of a sharp knife.
Quickly rinse the rice and drain it.
Pour the milk into a large heavy-based saucepan and add the vanilla pod. Bring to the boil then add the rice. Cover the saucepan and leave it to cook over a very low heat for about 30 minutes. Add the caster sugar, stirring it in quickly, cover and allow it to cook for another 5 minutes over a low heat.
Remove the vanilla pod. Pour the rice pudding into a serving dish and leave to cool, unless you prefer to eat it warm.

Confiture de lait ('milk jam')

Try a little experiment: without saying anything, put the pot of 'milk jam' on the table, leave a spoon lying near to it and observe the result. You can be sure every-one will be tempted!

Serves 4
Preparation time: 3 minutes
Cooking time: 4 hours

A large can of sweetened condensed milk

Pour the condensed milk into a jam pot. Put this in a deep flameproof casserole dish and add water to come up to the top of the jar, being careful not to let any overflow into the can. Place the container on top of the stove over low heat and leave it to simmer for about 4 hours. Add a little water at regular intervals to keep the water in the casserole at the same level. The milk will gradually turn a caramel colour. Remove from the heat, take out the jar and leave it to stand until it is lukewarm. Cover with clingfilm and store in a cool place.

Rice cake

Serves 4
Preparation time: 10 minutes
Cooking time: 50 minutes

1 non-stick flan tin

1 vanilla pod
175 g (6 oz) round grain (pudding) rice
1 litre (1¾ pints) milk
125 g (4 oz) caster sugar
2 eggs

For the caramel:
100 g (3½ oz) caster sugar
3 tablespoons water
2 drops of vinegar

Cut the vanilla pod in half lengthways with the point of a sharp knife.
Rinse the rice under running water and drain it.
Pour the milk into a large heavy-based saucepan and add the vanilla pod. Bring to the boil then add in the rice. Cover the saucepan and leave to cook over a very low heat for about 25 minutes. Preheat the oven to 180°C (350°F) Gas Mark 4.
To make the caramel, put the caster sugar and 3 tablespoons of water into a heavy-based saucepan and heat until the sugar has melted and the liquid has taken on a pale golden colour. Add the vinegar. Remove from the heat and put in 1 teaspoon of hot water. Pour the caramel into the tin, turning it as you do to make sure the bottom and sides are well coated.
Check whether the rice is cooked and add the caster sugar. Stir quickly, cover, and cook for another 5 minutes over a low heat. Remove from the heat and take out the vanilla pod. Whisk the eggs quickly in a bowl and then mix them into the rice and milk.
Pour the mixture into the caramelized mould and bake in the oven for about 20 minutes. Leave in the tin for a few minutes before turning out onto a rack to cool.

Confiture de lait – 'milk jam'

Creamy mousse with fromage blanc

Creamy mousse with fromage blanc

Serves 4
Preparation time: 5 minutes

200 ml (7 fl oz) whipping cream, chilled
60 g (2½ oz) icing sugar
200 g (7 oz) fromage blanc
1 vanilla pod

Pour the well-chilled whipping cream into a large bowl and whisk until it becomes frothy and increases in volume. Stir in the icing sugar, then fold in the fromage blanc with a spatula.
Cut the vanilla pod in half lengthways with the point of a sharp knife and scrape out the seeds with the point. Add the seeds to the fromage blanc.
Mix quickly and then pour into 4 small pots. Stand in a cool place for 30 minutes before serving.

Vanilla cream

Serves 4
Preparation time: 5 minutes
Cooking time: 5 minutes

4 tablespoons cornflour
500 ml (17 fl oz) milk
1 teaspoon vanilla essence
75 g (3 oz) caster sugar

Put the cornflour in a bowl and mix with a little cold milk.
Pour the remaining milk into a heavy-based saucepan and add the vanilla essence and caster sugar. Stir over medium heat until the sugar has melted and then bring to the boil.
Add the cornflour mixture to the hot milk and bring back to the boil, stirring all the time.
Take the saucepan off the heat and whisk strongly.
Put the cream into a bowl, leave until lukewarm and then serve in little pots.

Vanilla cream

Crème anglaise

It never goes out of fashion, it's a prime example of what a smooth, creamy dessert should be like. A wonderful sweet, with many qualities to recommend it … provided you keep a careful watch while cooking. It won't stand boiling or temperatures that are too high.

Serves 4–6
Preparation time: 5 minutes
Cooking time: 15 minutes

1 vanilla pod
1 litre (1¾ pints) milk
8 egg yolks
200 g (7 oz) caster sugar

Cut the vanilla pod in half lengthways with the point of a sharp knife. Pour the milk into a large heavy-based saucepan, add the vanilla pod and bring to simmering point. Remove the milk from the heat immediately, cover, and leave to infuse.
Put the egg yolks in a large bowl and gradually mix in the caster sugar, then whisk it so that the mixture becomes slightly lighter in colour.
Remove the vanilla pod from the milk, scrape out the seeds and add them to the milk. Gradually pour the vanilla-flavoured hot milk over the egg and sugar mixture, while stirring continuously with a wooden spoon.
Pour the custard into the saucepan and stand it once again over a low heat, stirring all the time. As soon as the custard thickens slightly and coats your spoon, remove the saucepan from the heat.
Pour the custard into a large bowl and cover with clingfilm. Leave it to stand until lukewarm then place in the refrigerator for an hour before serving.

Confectioner's custard

Serves 4
Preparation time: 5 minutes
Cooking time: 10 minutes

1 vanilla pod
250 ml (8 fl oz) milk
2 egg yolks
40 g (1½ oz) caster sugar
2 tablespoons cornflour

Cut the vanilla pod in half lengthways with the point of a sharp knife. Pour the milk into a heavy-based saucepan and add the vanilla pod. Heat gently over low heat.
Put the egg yolks and caster sugar in a large bowl and whisk rapidly.
Blend in the cornflour, mixing all the time. Remove the vanilla pod, scrape out the seeds with the point of the knife and add them to the milk. Gradually pour the vanilla-flavoured milk into the egg, sugar and cornflour mixture, stirring all the time.
Pour the mixture into the saucepan and bring it to the boil, stirring constantly. Lower the heat and cook for another 2 minutes over a low heat, stirring all the time. The custard will gradually thicken.
Pour it into a large bowl, cover with clingfilm and let it stand until it reaches room temperature. Place in the refrigerator for 30 minutes before serving.

Chantilly cream

Serves 4
Preparation time: 5 minutes

1 large bowl

300 ml (½ pint) whipping cream, well chilled
30 g (1¼ oz) icing sugar, sifted

Place the bowl in the freezer for 5 minutes.
Pour the very cold whipping cream into the iced
bowl, and whisk until it becomes frothy and
forms a good mass.
Add the icing sugar, folding it in with a spatula as
you do so.

Yogurt cake

Preparation time: 10 minutes
Cooking time: 30 minutes

1 round deep cake tin, about 26 cm (10 inches)
in diameter

100 g (3½ oz) soft unsalted butter, cut into
pieces, plus extra for greasing the tin
300 g (10 oz) plain flour
2 teaspoons baking powder
1 orange, unwaxed
150 g (5 oz) soft brown sugar
2 eggs
125 g (4 oz) creamy Greek yogurt
1 teaspoon vanilla essence

Preheat the oven to 180°C (350°F) Gas Mark 4.
Grease the cake tin generously and dust lightly
with flour.
Wash and dry the orange then finely grate the
rind.
Sift the flour and baking powder together into
a mixing bowl. Add the orange rind.
In a large bowl, carefully beat together the sugar
and pieces of butter. Add the eggs, yogurt and
vanilla essence. Now add the flour and orange
rind, mixing continuously.
Put this mixture into the cake tin, smoothing the
top with a spatula. Place it in the oven and bake
for about 30 minutes. Watch it carefully while it
is baking and if the top of the cake starts to
darken too much, cover with a sheet of
greaseproof paper.
Once the cake is out of the oven, wait 5 minutes
before turning it out onto a wire rack to cool.
Serve with well-chilled, creamy yogurt.

I don't wanna grow up!

Vanilla milk

Serves 1
Preparation time: 2 minutes

125 ml (4 fl oz) cold milk
½ teaspoon vanilla essence

Pour the cold milk and vanilla essence into a tall glass. Mix and serve.

You can, of course, also make this recipe the proper way. Cut half a vanilla pod in half lengthways with a sharp knife and scrape out the seeds with the point of the knife. Pour the milk into a saucepan and add the vanilla seeds and the half pod. Bring to simmering point. Remove the saucepan from the heat, cover, and leave to infuse for about 10 minutes. Take out the pod and place the vanilla-flavoured milk in the refrigerator.
Serve well chilled.

Honey milk

Serves 1
Preparation time: 2 minutes

2 teaspoons clear honey
125 ml (4 fl oz) cold milk

Put the honey in the bottom of a tall glass then add the cold milk.
You can mix the milk and honey together or leave them in two separate layers. If you decide on the latter, you will have a treat in store when you get to the bottom of the glass.

Milk with strawberry coulis

Serves 4
Preparation time: 5 minutes

100 g (3½ oz) very ripe strawberries
1 teaspoon vanilla essence
500 ml (17 fl oz) cold milk

Wash and hull the strawberries.
Put them in your liquidizer bowl, add vanilla essence and blend until smooth.
Pour a little strawberry coulis into each of four tall glasses. Gently add the cold milk and serve at once.

Tip: To make an attractive presentation, use clear glasses and pour the milk slowly against the sides to keep the two colours separate.

Banana milk shake

Papaya milk shake

Banana milk shake

Serves 2
Preparation time: 5 minutes

2 very ripe bananas
400 ml (14 fl oz) unsweetened condensed milk
1 teaspoon vanilla essence

Peel the bananas and slice them into rounds.
Put the milk, banana pieces and vanilla essence
into your liquidizer bowl. Blend until it reaches a
liquid, creamy consistency.
Pour into tall glasses.

Papaya milk shake

Serves 2
Preparation time: 5 minutes

1 very ripe papaya
400 ml (14 fl oz) cold milk

Peel the papaya, slice it in half, remove the seeds
and cut the flesh into large pieces. Place it in your
liquidizer bowl, add the milk and blend until
smooth.
Serve well chilled.

Milk shake with two milks

Serves 1
Preparation time: 5 minutes

50 ml (2 fl oz) condensed milk
50 ml (2 fl oz) fresh milk
5 ml (2 fl oz) water
1 teaspoon soft brown sugar
1 drop of orange flower water

Pour the condensed milk, fresh milk and water
into a bowl and add the sugar.
Add the orange flower water.
Whisk rapidly so that it becomes frothy, then
serve chilled in a tall glass.

Milk shake with powdered milk

Serves 1
Preparation time: 5 minutes

3 tablespoons powdered milk
150 ml (¼ pint) cold mineral water
1 dash of grenadine cordial

Put the powdered milk with the cold water and
grenadine into your liquidizer bowl and blend
thoroughly. Serve chilled in a tall glass.

Milk shake with two milks

Potatoes topped with fromage frais

Serves 4
Preparation time: 10 minutes
Cooking time: 30 minutes

8 large waxy potatoes
1 bay leaf
Freshly ground salt and pepper
1 small tub fromage frais
2 tablespoons chopped mixed herbs
(parsley, thyme, mint ...), or 2 crushed garlic
cloves, if you prefer

Wash the potatoes and put them in a casserole
filled with cold water. Add a bay leaf and plenty
of pepper.
Bring to the boil, then leave to simmer for about
30 minutes.
Drain the potatoes, then slice off the top of
each one and scoop out a hole with a small
spoon. Fill with a little fromage frais and serve
immediately.

Sweet dumplings

Serves 4
Preparation time: 25 minutes
Cooking time: 15 minutes

For the dumplings:
250 ml (8 fl oz) milk
100 g (3½ oz) unsalted butter, cut into pieces
Freshly ground salt and pepper
1 pinch of grated nutmeg
175 g (6 oz) flour
2 large eggs

For the sauce:
250 ml (8 fl oz) milk
250 ml (8 fl oz) crème fraîche
1 teaspoon honey
4 strands of saffron

To make the dumplings, put the milk and the pieces of butter into a heavy-based saucepan. Add salt and pepper and a little grated nutmeg. Heat gently until the butter melts, then add all the flour.
Blend with a spoon over a low heat for about 5 minutes to reduce the mixture to a fine dough then remove the saucepan from the heat and leave to cool. Give it a couple of stirs. Add the eggs one by one and mix them in.
Take a little of the dough with a dessert spoon and mould it into an oval-shaped dumpling with another spoon, then dust it lightly with flour. Repeat until the dough is used up.
Bring a large pan of water to the boil, add salt then gently put in the dumplings. When they rise to the surface (after about 3 minutes), remove from the pan with a slotted spoon.
To make the sauce, put the milk, crème fraîche and honey into a small heavy-based saucepan and warm over low heat. Add the strands of saffron. Cover, and leave to infuse for a few minutes. Strain the sauce, reheat, and serve hot over the dumplings.

Liquorice milk

Hot caramel milk

Liquorice milk

Serves 2
Preparation time: 2 minutes
Cooking time: 5 minutes

250 ml (8 fl oz) milk
1 stick dried liquorice root about 7 cm (3 inches)
long, or a stick of sweetshop liquorice

Put the milk into a heavy-based saucepan and
add the liquorice stick. Bring to simmering point
and heat gently, uncovered, for about 5 minutes.
Leave to infuse for a few seconds, strain, then
serve hot.
The amount of liquorice may be halved. You will
then get a milder flavoured milk.

Tip: If you use a stick of liquorice bought from
a sweetshop, instead of a liquorice root, it will
cook much more quickly and taste sweeter.

Hot caramel milk

Serves 2
Preparation time: 5 minutes
Cooking time: 5 minutes

250 ml (8 fl oz) milk
4 brown sugar cubes
2 tablespoons water

Pour the milk into a saucepan and heat it gently
until it simmers.
Take the pan off the heat, cover, and keep warm.
Put the sugar cubes into a small heavy-based
saucepan, add the 2 tablespoons of water and
heat until the sugar melts and the caramel takes
on a lovely golden colour
Pour into two tall glasses, add the milk and serve.

Hot vanilla milk

Serves 2 people
Preparation time: 5 minutes
Cooking time: 5 minutes

½ vanilla pod
300 ml (½ pint) milk

Cut the vanilla pod in half lengthways with a
sharp knife and scrape out the seeds with the
point of the knife.
Pour the milk into a heavy-based saucepan and
add the vanilla pod and the seeds. Heat gently
until it simmers.
Remove from the heat, cover, and leave to infuse
for 10 minutes. Remove the vanilla pod from the
pan and serve.

Hot almond-flavoured milk

Serves 2
Preparation time: 5 minutes
Preparation time: 5 minutes

250 ml (8 fl oz) milk
2 tablespoons ground almonds
1 teaspoon vanilla essence

Pour the milk into a small heavy-based saucepan
and add the ground almonds and vanilla essence.
Heat gently, allow to simmer for a few minutes,
and remove from the heat. Leave to stand until
lukewarm, pour into two glasses and serve
immediately.

Hot vanilla milk

Hot milk with marshmallow

Serves 2
Preparation time: 5 minutes
Cooking time: 5 minutes

2–3 marshmallows
250 ml (8 fl oz) milk

Cut the marshmallows into small pieces with a
pair of scissors.
Gently heat the milk in a small heavy-based
saucepan.
Divide the marshmallow between two tall glasses.
Pour in the hot milk, mix and serve.

Tip: The marshmallow will appear on the surface
in little bits. Part of it will have melted and the
other part will be floating, so you can play
around with the colours: pink, yellow, white, etc.

on the farm

Your childhood, just like the place you come from, marks you forever! Childhood for me will always be associated with farm holidays. Mild summer evenings, scented with lime; milking time in the cowshed; flights of swallows, the metallic clink of milk churns being carried down to the cellar.

My earliest pleasures? Giant slices of buttered bread and jam dipped in a big bowl of milky coffee, cake with the skin of the milk wizened like an old apple.

'Go on with you, you little scamp!' says the voice of Marcelline, but the trouble was she would end up eating the lot, the greedy thing! Treats stolen secretly from the kitchen: cream hearts, whey still running from the soft white cheese. Just dip the tip of the finger in …

Oh! those food-gathering forays in the garden, in the forest, along the river's edge! White raspberries still moist with dew, pockets full of hazelnuts.

Once home, we would eat like wolves, welcomed for once at the grown-ups' table: blanquette of veal, chicken in crème fraîche …

You'll have a little more, won't you children?

Spicy hot chocolate

Spicy hot chocolate

Serves 4
Preparation time: 5 minutes
Cooking time: 8 minutes

125 g (4 oz) dark chocolate, 70% cocoa solids
100 ml (3½ oz) water
2 pinches of ground cinnamon
500 ml (17 fl oz) milk
1 teaspoon vanilla essence

Break the dark chocolate into pieces.
Pour the water into a saucepan and add the
cinnamon. Bring to simmering point then add
the milk and leave to heat gently. Add the vanilla
essence, mix rapidly and remove from the heat.
Put the pieces of chocolate into the hot milk and
whisk for a few moments until the chocolate
melts and becomes slightly frothy. Serve
immediately.

Café au lait (milky coffee)

Serves 2 large bowls, or very large mugs
Preparation time: 10 minutes
Cooking time: 3 minutes

4 sugar cubes
200 ml (7 fl oz) coffee
200 ml (7 fl oz) milk

Put two sugar cubes in each bowl.
Brew your coffee then gently heat the milk.
Pour the hot coffee into the bowls then add
the hot milk. Stir slowly and enjoy.

Note: If you want to dunk your croissant,
be our guest!

Café au lait

Top of the milk

Cake with the skin of the milk

Serves 4
Preparation time: 15 minutes
Cooking time: 40 minutes

1 deep round cake tin about 18 cm (7 inches)
in diameter

1.2 kg (2½ lb) cooking apples
60 g (2½ oz) caster sugar
1 teaspoon vanilla essence
30 g (1¼ oz) butter, plus extra for greasing the tin
flour, for dusting
3 tablespoons milk skin or thick crème fraîche
3 eggs
3 teaspoons potato flour
1 tablespoon rum

Peel and quarter the apples and remove the cores and pips. Cut the quarters into large pieces and put in a big saucepan. Add 1 tablespoon of water, the caster sugar and the vanilla essence. Mix and leave to simmer until the apple quarters are just soft. Remove from the heat, allow to cool a little, then mash the apples with a fork and drain away any juice.
Grease the tin and lightly dust with flour.
Preheat the oven to 180°C (350°F) Gas Mark 4.
Melt the butter in a small saucepan over a low heat.
Whisk the milk skin and eggs in a large bowl. Add the melted butter then fold this mixture into the stewed apples.
Mix the potato flour with 2 tablespoons of water and add to the apples, mixing it in carefully.
Pour into the prepared tin and bake in the oven for about 30 minutes. Mix the rum with 1 tablespoon of water and sprinkle over the cake before serving it lukewarm.

Note: The skin of the milk was very often used in the old days in country cooking; it was a delicious way of using up the skin that formed when the fresh milk from the cow had been boiled.

Top of the milk

Preparation time: 5 minutes
Cooking time: 5 minutes
Standing time: overnight

1 litre (1¾ pints) milk

Pour the milk into a large saucepan and bring to the boil.
Remove from the heat immediately and leave to cool.
Put the saucepan in the refrigerator overnight. Lift off the skin that has formed on the surface of the milk with a slotted spoon.

Apple tart with 'milk jam'

Preparation time: 15 minutes
Resting time: 1 hour
Cooking time: 30 minutes

1 flan dish, about 26 cm (10 inches) in diameter

For the rich shortcrust pastry:
250 g (8 oz) plain flour
125 g (4 oz) soft unsalted butter, cut in pieces
1 egg yolk
pinch of salt
50 ml (2 fl oz) water

For the topping:
4 Cox's orange pippins
1 pinch ground cinnamon
2 tablespoons lemon juice
250 g (8 oz) 'milk jam' (see page 18)

To make the pastry, put the flour into a large
bowl and make a well in the centre. Add the
pieces of butter and rub them in with your
fingertips. Make another well, pour in the egg
yolk and salt and mix them in lighty, adding
the water gradually. Do not add the water all
at once, you may not need all of it to form
the dough.
Draw the pastry into a ball and wrap it in
clingfilm. Put it in a cool place or refrigerator
for 1 hour.
Preheat the oven to 180°C (350°F) Gas Mark 4.
Peel and quarter the apples, remove the cores and
pips then cut the quarters into slices, put in a dish
and sprinkle over the ground cinnamon. Pour over
the lemon juice and mix.
Grease and lightly flour your flan dish then line it
with the pastry. Lightly prick the base of the tart
with a fork, spread over the 'milk jam' and
arrange the apple slices on top.
Cover with a sheet of kitchen foil and bake in the
oven for 20 minutes.
Remove the foil and continue baking for a further
10 minutes.
Leave to cool.

Tip: If you are in a hurry, you need not chill
the pastry for an hour. You can roll it out
straight away.

Cream hearts

Soft white cheese with crème fraîche

Cream hearts

Serves 4
Preparation time: 10 minutes
Standing time: overnight

4 small heart-shaped moulds
4 squares of muslin, to line the moulds

500 g (1 lb) thick crème fraîche,
45% fat content
4 very fresh egg whites
pinch of salt
30 g (1¼ oz) icing sugar

For the topping:
100 ml (3½ fl oz) whipping cream, chilled
4 teaspoons brown sugar
red berries

To make the hearts, pour the very cold crème fraîche into a large bowl and whip it.
Put the egg whites into a large bowl, add a small pinch of salt and whisk them with an electric whisk until they are stiff and stand up in peaks. Add the icing sugar and continue whisking for a few moments.
Gently fold the egg whites gradually into the whipped crème fraîche, using a spatula. Line each mould with a small square of muslin then fill it with the creamy mixture. Stand overnight in a cool place or refrigerator to firm up.
The next day, serve the hearts with a little lightly whipped cream poured over them. Sprinkle with brown sugar and add a few berries (raspberries, blackcurrants, redcurrants or blackberries).

Tip: The muslin is recommended but not strictly necessary for this recipe.

Soft white cheese with crème fraîche

Serves 4
Preparation time: 5 minutes

400 g (13 oz) strained soft white cheese
300 ml (½ pint) crème fraîche
demerara sugar

Divide the soft white cheese between 4 bowls. Stir the crème fraîche to loosen it and pour into a small jug.
Serve the bowls of soft white cheese together with the jug of crème fraîche and sugar, and let people help themselves according to taste.

Egg custard

Serves 4–6
Preparation time: 10 minutes
Cooking time: 30 minutes

1 charlotte mould

knob of butter, for greasing
500 ml (17 fl oz) milk
½ teaspoon vanilla essence
2 eggs
100 g (3½ oz) caster sugar

Preheat the oven to 180°C (350°F) Gas Mark 4. Grease the mould.
Pour the milk and vanilla essence into a heavy-based saucepan and bring to the boil. Remove the saucepan from the heat and cover. Break the eggs into a large bowl, add the caster sugar and whisk rapidly. Slowly pour in the boiling vanilla-flavoured milk, while continuing to mix. Whisk rapidly then pour the mixture into the mould. Put the mould into an ovenproof dish or roasting tin and fill with just simmering water to two thirds up the mould. Place in the hot oven for about 30 minutes. The surface of the dish will become slightly golden. If it begins to get too brown, reduce the oven temperature a little. Remove from the oven and let stand to cool. Serve when lukewarm.

Egg custard

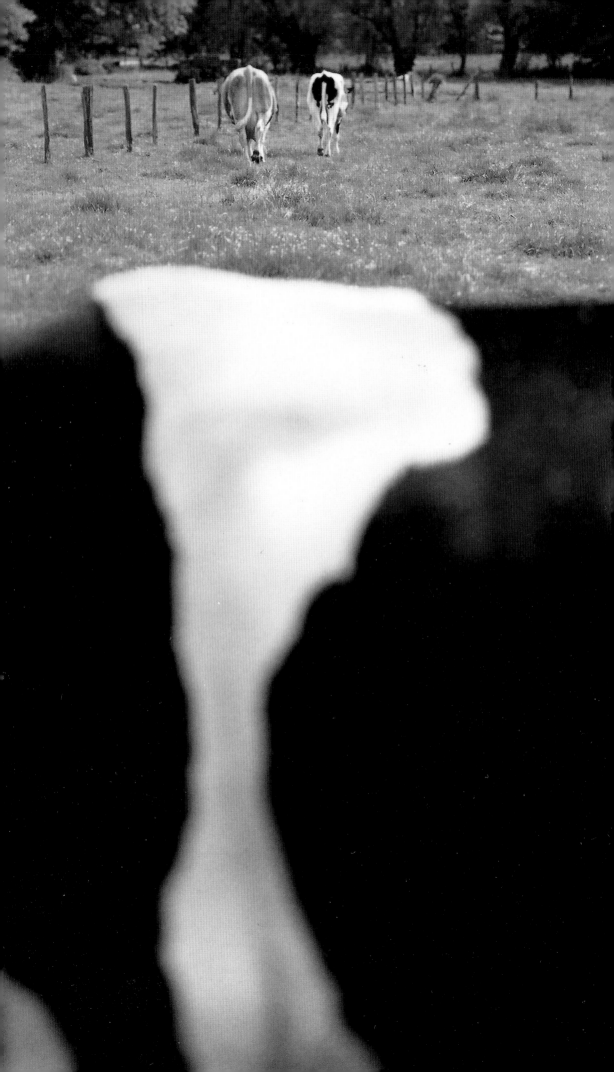

Little pots of yogurt with chocolate

Pots of whipped petits-suisses

Little pots of yogurt with chocolate

Serves 4
Preparation time: 5 minutes
Cooking time: 5 minutes

100 g (3½ oz) dark chocolate
50 ml (2 fl oz) milk
50 ml (2 fl oz) crème fraîche
4 small natural yogurts

Break the chocolate into small pieces and put in a large bowl. Alternatively you can grate it with a coarse grater.
Pour the milk and crème fraîche into a small saucepan and gently heat. Cover the chocolate with this mixture. Leave to rest for one or two minutes then stir vigorously. The chocolate will melt and become mixed with the milk and crème fraîche.
Serve the yogurts topped with this chocolate cream.

Pots of whipped petits-suisses

Serves 4
Preparation time: 5 minutes

4 little individual pots

6 petits-suisses
2 tablespoons milk
4 tablespoons caster sugar
½ teaspoon vanilla essence
1 tablespoon rum

Pour the petits-suisses, milk, caster sugar, vanilla essence and rum into a large bowl. Whip until the mixture becomes frothy, then spoon into the little pots.
Serve chilled.

Fromage blanc with wild strawberries

Redcurrants with whipped cream

Fromage blanc with wild strawberries

Serves 4
Preparation time: 10 minutes
Standing time: overnight

4 small soft white cheese pots and 4 squares of muslin (see Tip)

150 ml (¼ pint) whipping cream, well chilled
30 g (1¼ oz) icing sugar
350 g (12 oz) smooth fromage blanc,
40% fat content
handful of wild strawberries

Pour the whipping cream into a large bowl, add the icing sugar and whisk to increase the volume. Gradually fold in the fromage blanc.
Put a square of muslin into each pot. Fill it with the creamy mixture, fold the muslin over the top and put in a cool place or refrigerator overnight. Turn out onto plates and serve garnished with a few wild strawberries.

Tip: The muslin is recommended but not essential.

Redcurrants with whipped cream

Serves 2–4 people
Preparation time: 10 minutes

300 ml (1½ pint) whipping cream, chilled
30 g (1¼ oz) icing sugar
300 g (10 oz) redcurrants

Place a large bowl in the freezer for 5 minutes. Pour the well-chilled whipping cream into the iced bowl and whisk, using an electric whisk, until it becomes frothy and increases in volume. Add the icing sugar, mixing it in with a spatula. Put back in a cool place or refrigerator until you are ready to serve.
Carefully rinse the redcurrants, let them drain for a few minutes, then arrange in a bowl. Present the bowls of whipped cream and redcurrants together.

Marcelline's soft white cheese and raspberry crush

Serves 4
Preparation time: 5 minutes

125 g (4 oz) raspberries
60 g (2½ oz) icing sugar
4 small soft white cheeses

Quickly rinse the raspberries and drain them. Put the raspberries into a large bowl, add the icing sugar and mix thoroughly, mashing with the back of a spoon. Pour this crush into a pot or bowl.
Serve the cheeses, chilled, accompanied by the raspberry crush, with everyone helping themself from the pot.

Marcelline's soft white cheese and raspberry crush

Whipped cream with wild blackberries

Serves 4
Preparation time: 10 minutes

200 ml (7 fl oz) whipping cream, well chilled
1 tablespoon brandy
2 tablespoons icing sugar
250 g (8 oz) blackberries

Pour the whipping cream and brandy into a large bowl, and whisk together until the cream clings to the whisk. Add the sugar. Pick over and wash the wild blackberries, and arrange them in little individual bowls. Cover the fruit with whipped cream. Serve immediately.

French toast with white raspberries

Serves 4
Preparation time: 5 minutes
Cooking time: 8 minutes

250 g (8 oz) white raspberries, or red if necessary
2 eggs
40 g (1½ oz) caster sugar
300 ml (1½ pints) milk
1 teaspoon vanilla essence
knob of butter
oil
8 slices of stale brioche

Briefly rinse and drain the raspberries. Break the eggs into a bowl and add 1 tablespoon of caster sugar. Whisk quickly with a fork then pour into a shallow dish.
Pour the milk into a second shallow dish.
Mix together the rest of the caster sugar and the vanilla essence.
Heat the butter and 1 tablespoon of oil in a frying pan.
Quickly dip the slices of brioche into the beaten eggs then into the milk. Cook them over medium heat until they become golden then turn the slices over and let them cook for another one or two minutes.
Serve the slices of brioche hot, sprinkled with caster sugar and accompanied by the raspberries.

Chicken in crème fraîche

Serves 4
Preparation time: 10 minutes
Cooking time: 30 minutes

Freshly ground salt and pepper
1 chicken weighing 1.2 kg (2½ lb),
cut into pieces
oil
knob of butter
400 g (13 oz) cultivated mushrooms
3½ tablespoons calvados
500 ml (17 fl oz) thick crème fraîche

Season the chicken with salt and pepper. Heat
1 tablespoon of oil and the butter in a flameproof
casserole. Put in the chicken pieces and let them
brown on all sides, turning them over from time
to time. Add 2 tablespoons of water and cover.
Allow them to cook over medium heat for about
15 minutes. Rinse the mushrooms quickly and dry
them before cutting into slices. Heat 1 tablespoon
of oil in a non-stick pan and fry the mushrooms
for a few minutes.
When the chicken pieces are cooked, remove
them from the casserole. (First, test that the juices
run clear when the flesh is pierced deeply by a
sharp skewer.)
Heat the calvados in a small saucepan, pour it
over the chicken pieces and quickly flambé.
Pour the crème fraîche into the casserole, stir
and heat gently. Return the chicken pieces to
the casserole, add the mushrooms together
with some pepper and mix well.
Serve immediately from the casserole.

Blanquette of veal

Serves 4
Preparation time: 15 minutes
Cooking time: 1 hour

200 ml (7 fl oz) dry white wine
2 onions, peeled, 1 studded with 2 cloves
1 bouquet garni
1 garlic clove, peeled
freshly ground salt and pepper
1 kg (2 lb) veal (breast, middle-cut breast,
shoulder), cut into large pieces
2 carrots, sliced into rounds
50 g (2 oz) butter
40 g (1½ oz) flour
125 g (4 oz) cultivated mushrooms
1 very fresh egg yolk
2 tablespoons lemon juice
3 tablespoons thick crème fraîche

Pour the white wine and about 1½ litres (2½ pints)
of cold water into a flameproof casserole. Add
the 2 onions, bouquet garni and the peeled garlic
clove. Season, then bring to the boil over medium
heat. Add the pieces of veal and slices of carrot.
The liquid should cover the meat. Lower the heat,
cover and simmer for about 20 minutes. Remove
any scum with a slotted spoon. Remove the veal
pieces and drain. Set aside 300 ml (½ pint) of the
stock and leave the rest in the casserole.
Melt 30 g (1¼ oz) of the butter in a high-sided
frying pan, put in the veal pieces, sprinkle with
flour and let them brown. Slowly pour in the
300 ml (½ pint) reserved stock, mixing it in with
a spoon. Leave it to simmer, covered, for about
20 minutes.
Peel the mushrooms and halve or quarter the
largest ones.
Melt the remaining butter in a pan and fry the
mushrooms for a few minutes. Add them to the
veal pieces and let them simmer for a few
minutes until all is cooked through. Drain the
meat and vegetables and keep them warm.
Reduce the remaining cooking stock for 2 or
3 minutes then remove the casserole from
the heat.
In a bowl, mix the egg yolk with the lemon juice
and crème fraîche, then pour into the casserole.
Season to taste and stir till the sauce thickens.
Serve the veal and vegetables with the sauce,
accompanied by plain rice.

Roast veal with milk

Serves 4–6
Preparation time: 10 minutes
Cooking time: 1 hour

1 veal joint (shoulder, leg),
about 1.2 kg (2½ lb)
1 litre (1¾ pints) milk
freshly ground salt and pepper
2 sage leaves
2 sprigs of thyme

Preheat the oven to 180°C (350°F) Gas Mark 4.
Place the veal joint in an ovenproof casserole,
pour over the milk and season with salt and
pepper. Put in the sage leaves and sprigs of
thyme.
Put the casserole in the oven uncovered. Leave
it to cook for about 50 minutes, checking every
now and then to see how it is doing. Turn the
joint of veal over and stir with a spoon to break
up the skin that will have formed on the milk's
surface. Preheat the grill. When the joint is
ready, remove from the casserole, wipe it with
kitchen paper and place under the grill for
about 8 minutes to caramelize the outside.
Strain the cooking milk and serve it with the
roast.

Gratin savoyard

Gratin savoyard

Serves 4–6
Preparation time: 15 minutes
Cooking time: 40 minutes

1 gratin dish

1 garlic clove, peeled and halved
50 g (2 oz) butter, for greasing and topping
750 g (1½ lb) potatoes
2 onions
freshly ground salt and pepper
nutmeg
500 ml (17 fl oz) milk
125g (4 oz) comté or gruyère cheese, grated

Preheat the oven to 180°C (350°F) Gas Mark 4.
Rub the inside of the gratin dish with the garlic
clove then grease it with a knob of butter.
Peel the potatoes, rinse and dry them carefully,
cut into slices. Put the potatoes into a large bowl,
add a little salt and a generous amount of pepper,
sprinkle with a little grated nutmeg and mix.
Peel and thinly slice the onions.
Warm the milk.
Sprinkle three-quarters of the grated cheese over
the potatoes, add the onions, then pour over the
milk. Mix together and transfer to the gratin dish.
Sprinkle with the remaining grated cheese and
knobs of butter. Bake in the oven for 40 minutes.

Gratin dauphinois

Serves 4–6 people
Preparation time: 15 minutes
Cooking time: 35 minutes

1 gratin dish

1 garlic clove, peeled and halved
knob of butter
750 g (1½ lb) potatoes
freshly ground salt and pepper
400 ml (14 fl oz) milk
200 ml (7 fl oz) crème fraîche

Preheat the oven to 180°C (350°F) Gas Mark 4.
Rub the inside of the gratin dish with the garlic
clove and grease it with the knob of butter.
Peel the potatoes, rinse and dry them carefully
and cut into very thin slices. Put them in a large
bowl, add a little salt and a generous amount of
pepper and mix well together.
Warm the milk.
Place the slices of potato in the gratin dish. In a
large bowl, mix the crème fraîche with the warm
milk. Whisk lightly then pour it over the gratin.
Bake in the oven for about 35 minutes. At the
end of the cooking time, the gratin should be
golden on top and the point of a knife should
slide in easily.

Real mashed potato

Serves 4
Preparation time: 15 minutes
Cooking time: 25 minutes

1 potato masher or potato ricer

1 kg (2 lb) floury potatoes
freshly ground salt and pepper
200 ml (7 fl oz) milk
50 g (2 oz) butter, cut into pieces

Rinse the potatoes and put them, unpeeled, in a large saucepan. Cover with cold water and add salt. Cook for about 20 minutes. To check whether they are cooked, stick a knife into one of the potatoes to see whether it slides in easily. Heat the milk in a small saucepan, remove from the heat and cover.
Drain and skin the potatoes, then mash them with the potato masher or ricer. Put the mashed potato in a saucepan and let it dry out over a very low heat for 2 to 3 minutes while stirring with a spoon. Add the pieces of butter, continuing to stir all the time. Slowly pour in the hot milk while continuing to stir.
Taste and adjust the seasoning if necessary.

Tip: You can, if you like, flavour your mashed potato with curry, allspice or nutmeg.

Potato soup with Ribot milk

You may be able to bring back this type of milk from a trip to Brittany.

Serves 4
Preparation time: 10 minutes
Cooking time: 35 minutes

750 g (1½ lb) floury potatoes
1 bay leaf
1 sprig of thyme
freshly ground salt and pepper
600ml (1 pint) Ribot milk

Rinse the potatoes and put them, unpeeled, in a large saucepan of cold water. Add the bayleaf and thyme. Simmer for about 30 minutes. To check whether they are cooked, slide the blade of a knife into one of the potatoes. If the blade goes in easily, stop cooking and remove from the heat. Drain and skin the potatoes and mash them with a potato masher or ricer. Adjust the seasoning to taste. Serve hot.
The Ribot milk can be served in a jug, and added by each person according to taste.

Note: If you can't get any Ribot milk, use hot full-fat milk, which you can flavour with a pinch of nutmeg or another spice of your choice.

Real mashed potato

Chestnut purée with milk

Serves 4
5 minutes preparation time
10 minutes cooking time

100 ml (3½ fl oz) water
50 g (2 oz) powdered milk
400 g (13 oz) chestnut purée
knob of butter
2 tablespoons thick crème fraîche
pinch of salt
freshly ground pepper
1 tablespoon caster sugar

Heat the water in a saucepan.
Add the powdered milk and mix.
Lower the heat and add the chestnut purée
spoonful by spoonful until it has absorbed the
milk. Add the butter and crème fraîche, then
salt and pepper to taste. Add the caster sugar
and mix well. Cover, and leave it to heat gently
for 5 to 8 minutes.

Fromage blanc with herbs

Serves 4
Preparation time: 10 minutes

500 g (1 lb) fromage blanc, chilled
2 tablespoons chopped parsley
2 tablespoons chopped chervil
1 tablespoon chopped tarragon
1 shallot, chopped
1 tablespoon olive oil
½ tablespoon vinegar (preferably cider)
freshly ground salt and pepper

Put the fromage blanc into a large bowl.
Add the chopped parsley, chervil, tarragon
and shallot. Mix well then pour in the olive
oil and vinegar. Add salt and pepper to taste.
Serve the fromage blanc with herbs at room
temperature in winter and chilled in summer,
with a nice crusty baguette or a thick slice of
rye bread.

Tip: Make this recipe in advance so that the
herbs and seasonings can develop their flavours.

brunches for
lazy mornings

Long live lazy mornings, lingering in bed with a book at hand – poetry
perhaps, or a traveller's tale. Oh, the temptations of those little luxuries
eaten straight from the dish: caramel custard or vanilla porridge … and to
crown these epicurean delights, some spicy milk tea. What's next on the
menu? A milky brunch!

Bowl of cereal with milk and dried fruit

Serves 2
Preparation time: 5 minutes

4 prunes
4 dried apricots
60 g (2½ oz) breakfast cereal
milk
1 tablespoon dried papaya pieces
1 tablespoon freshly chopped hazelnuts
2 tablespoons thick crème fraîche

Slit the prunes and remove the stones.
Cut the prunes and dried apricots into strips.
Put the cereal into 2 bowls, and cover with
cold milk. Add the prunes, apricots and diced
papaya. Sprinkle over the chopped hazelnuts,
add 1 tablespoon of crème fraîche to each bowl
and eat immediately.

Home-made muesli

Cereal flakes with honey

Home-made muesli

Serves 2
Preparation time: 10 minutes
Standing time: overnight

50 g (2 oz) cereal flakes (wheat, barley or oats)
2 apples
50 g (2 oz) fruit in season (strawberries, apricots,
figs, oranges, etc.)
1 tablespoon freshly chopped walnuts or
hazelnuts
4 tablespoons honey
1 teaspoon sesame seeds
milk

Put the cereal flakes into a large bowl, cover them
with water and leave them to swell in a cool place
overnight.
Wash and grate the apples. Wash the other fruit
and cut it into small pieces.
Mix together the cereal flakes, grated apple,
pieces of fresh fruit and chopped nuts. Add the
honey and sesame seeds. Pour on a little milk,
mix and serve.

Cereal flakes with honey

Serves 2
Preparation time: 5 minutes
Standing time: overnight

50 g (2 oz) mixed cereal flakes
(wheat, barley, oats)
milk
4 tablespoons honey
1 pinch of ground cinnamon
2 tablespoons raisins

Put the cereal flakes in a bowl and cover them
with water. Leave to stand in a cool place, or
the refrigerator, overnight.
Next day, pour a little milk over the cereals
then add the honey. Sprinkle a pinch of ground
cinnamon over the top, add the raisins, then
mix and serve.

Corn flakes just as they are

Serves 2
Preparation time: 1 minute

milk
2 bowls of corn flakes
Demerara or muscovado sugar

Pour the cold milk over the corn flakes, sprinkle
a little sugar on top and eat.

Corn flakes with yogurt

Serves 2
Preparation time: 5 minutes

60 g (2½ oz) corn flakes
200 g (7 oz) yogurts
juice of 2 squeezed oranges
1 tablespoon Demerara sugar

Divide the corn flakes between two bowls.
Pour the yogurt and orange juice into a large
bowl and mix. Cover the corn flakes with this
mixture. Sprinkle brown sugar over and eat.

Corn flakes just as they are

Petits-suisses with orange

Serves 2
Preparation time: 5 minutes

4 petits-suisses
2 tablespoons caster sugar
2 tablespoons milk
2 oranges

Put the petits-suisses into a large bowl.
Add the caster sugar and mix. Pour in the
milk and whisk to obtain a creamy mixture.
Peel the oranges, splitting the first one into
whole segments and cutting the segments
from the second into small pieces. Mix the
orange pieces with the petits-suisses. Spoon
into 2 small dishes and arrange the orange
segments on top. Serve chilled.

Yogurt with honey

Serves 2
Preparation time: 1 minute

2 tablespoons flower honey
2 creamy yogurts, Greek or Greek-style

Spoon the honey over the yogurts and mix.

Vanilla porridge

Serves 2
Preparation time: 5 minutes
Cooking time: 4 minutes

400 ml (14 fl oz) milk
1 teaspoon vanilla essence
pinch of salt
4 tablespoons pre-cooked oat flakes
knob of butter
Demerara sugar
100 ml (3½ fl oz) cold milk, or single cream

Pour the milk into a heavy-based saucepan.
Add the vanilla sugar and a pinch of salt then
bring to the boil. Pour in the oat flakes. Allow
to cook for about 2 minutes over a high heat,
stirring all the time with a spoon.
Pour into small bowls. Put a knob of butter into
each bowl and sprinkle a little brown sugar over.
Serve with well-chilled milk or cream. Add some
fresh fruit, like blueberries, if you have any.

Fromage frais with fresh fruit

Serves 2
Preparation time: 5 minutes

2 very ripe apricots
1 very ripe peach
2 pots creamy fromage frais,
about 125 g (4 oz) each
1 teaspoon vanilla essence

Wash and dry the fruit. Peel the peach if you
wish. Cut each piece of fruit into two and remove
the stones, then cut them into small pieces.
Put the fromage frais into a large bowl, add
the vanilla essence and mix.
Spoon the mixture into 2 small bowls. Add
the pieces of fresh fruit and serve.

Caramel custard

Serves 2–4 people
Preparation time: 5 minutes
Cooking time: 30 minutes

1 flan tin, non-stick preferably
1 deep ovenproof dish or roasting tin

500 ml (17 fl oz) milk
100 g (3½ oz) caster sugar
1 vanilla essence
4 eggs

For the caramel:
4 tablespoons caster sugar
2 tablespoons water

Preheat the oven to 150°C (300°F) Gas Mark 2.
To make the caramel, put the caster sugar and
the water into a small heavy-based saucepan.
Heat until the mixture turns a golden caramel
colour. Pour into the flan tin, turning it as you
do so to make sure the caramel covers the
whole base of the flan tin.
To make the custard, pour the milk into a
heavy-based saucepan. Add the caster sugar
and vanilla essence and bring gently to the boil.
Take it off the heat straight away, and stir to
make sure the sugar has dissolved.
Put a kettle of water on to boil.
Break the eggs into a large bowl and whisk
with a fork. Gradually pour in the hot milk
while continuing to mix.
Pour the custard into the caramelized flan tin
and place in the dish or roasting tin. Put the
bain-marie onto the oven shelf and then slide
out the shelf a little way and pour in boiling
water to two-thirds up the side of the flan tin.
Gently slide the shelf back and bake the caramel
custard for about 30 minutes. Leave it to cool
before turning out.

Cappuccino

Serves 2
Preparation time: 5 minutes
Cooking time: 3 minutes

2 tablespoons coffee,
ground finely for espresso
200 ml (7 fl oz) milk
2 pinches of cocoa powder

Prepare 2 large cups of espresso coffee.
Warm the milk in a saucepan then whisk it
with a small whisk until it becomes very frothy.
Immediately pour the frothy milk into the cups
of coffee, taking care to pour the milk in before
the froth. Using a small spoon to hold back the
froth will help you to do this.
Sprinkle a little cocoa powder over the top and
drink.

Spicy milk tea

Serves 2
Preparation time: 5 minutes
Cooking time: 10 minutes

500 ml (17 fl oz) still mineral water
8 cardamom pods
2 cloves
1 piece of cinnamon stick, 3 cm long
(about an inch)
200 ml (7 fl oz) milk
6 teaspoons caster sugar
3 teaspoons black tea leaves

Pour the water into a saucepan. Add the
cardamom pods, cloves and cinnamon stick.
Bring to the boil. Cover and leave to simmer
over a low heat for 5 minutes. Add the milk
and caster sugar and bring back to a simmer.
Immediately remove the saucepan from the heat
and stir in the tea leaves. Cover, and leave to
infuse for 2–3 minutes, then strain before serving.

Viennese coffee

Serves 2
Preparation time: 5 minutes
Cooking time: 3 minutes

50 ml (2 fl oz) whipping cream, chilled
1 pinch of ground cinnamon
200 ml (7 fl oz) milk
2 cups of coffee
Demerara sugar

Pour the whipping cream into a bowl and stir
in the pinch of ground cinnamon. Whip the
cream until it thickens, but not too much.
Gently heat the milk in a small saucepan.
Pour the hot coffee into 2 large cups. Add
the hot milk and mix. Add sugar according to
taste then top with a spoonful of the whipped
cream and cinnamon.

Orchata

Serves 2
Preparation time: 5 minutes
Cooking time: 5 minutes

500 ml (17 fl oz) milk
100 ml whipping cream
½ teaspoon bitter almond essence
2 tablespoons caster sugar

Pour the milk and cream into a saucepan and
heat gently, stirring once or twice. Bring to
simmering point then remove from the heat.
Add the bitter almond essence and stir in the
sugar. Leave to become lukewarm.
Serve lukewarm or iced.

Blinis

Serves 2
Preparation time: 10 minutes
Cooking time: 4 minutes per blini

100 g (3½ oz) plain flour
1 egg
125 ml (4 fl oz) milk
pinch of salt
2 egg whites
knob of butter
thick crème fraîche

Put the flour into a large bowl and make a well
in the centre. Add the egg and mix in, then
gradually incorporate the milk, beating to remove
any lumps.
Put the egg whites in another bowl, add a pinch
of salt, and beat with an electric whisk until they
stand up in peaks.
Fold the egg whites into the batter little by little.
Lightly oil a blini pan, or small frying pan, and put
in a small ladleful of batter. Let it cook over a low
heat for about 2 minutes on each side then
continue to cook the other blinis.
Serve immediately with the thick crème fraîche.

Cucumber salad with yogurt and mint

Serves 2
Preparation time: 10 minutes
Chilling time: 2 hours

1 small cucumber
500 ml (17 fl oz) runny yogurt
1 tablespoon chopped parsley
2 tablespoons chopped fresh mint,
plus mint sprigs to garnish
freshly ground salt and pepper

Peel the cucumber and cut into small dice.
Put the cucumber into a bowl and mix in the
yogurt, parsley and mint leaves. Season to taste
and leave to chill in the refrigerator for at least
2 hours before serving. Serve, garnished with
mint sprigs.

Scrambled eggs with Parmesan cheese

Serves 2
Preparation time: 5 minutes
Cooking time: 5 minutes

4 eggs
1 tablespoon milk
salt
small pinch of ground cinnamon
small pinch of ground allspice
½ tablespoon oil
knob of butter
50 g (2 oz) freshly grated Parmesan cheese

Break the eggs into a large bowl. Add the milk,
a little salt, the pinch of ground cinnamon and
the pinch of ground allspice. Whisk the eggs
with a fork.
Heat the oil and butter in a frying pan. Pour in
the beaten eggs and heat slowly, continuing to
stir with a spatula.
As soon as they begin to stick to the base and
sides, draw the eggs towards the centre of the
pan. The consistency should remain creamy.
Remove the frying pan from the heat, fold in
the grated Parmesan and serve immediately.

Bruschetta with mozzarella

Serves 2
Preparation time: 5 minutes
Cooking time: 3–4 minutes

2 portions of mozzarella, 125 g (4 oz) each
4 slices pain de campagne (or French bread)
1 jar sun-dried tomato paste in oil
freshly ground pepper

Preheat the grill.
Drain the mozzarella and pat dry with kitchen
paper. Cut into thick slices.
Spread each slice of bread with a thin layer of
sun-dried tomato paste.
Arrange the slices of mozzarella on top, add
pepper and place them under the hot grill for
about 3–4 minutes. Wait until the mozzarella
melts and the bread becomes slightly golden at
the edges before removing from the grill and
serving.

tv suppers

Boredom is the mother of invention in the kitchen. Time for solitary pleasures: tapioca with coconut, semolina with milk and lemon … quick … no one's looking, you can have anything you fancy! Condensed milk spread on a slice of bread, 'milk jam', coconut drops …

Or, a spoon shared between two people in love, delectable flavours and giggles all jumbled up. Memories of holidays, vaporetto mousse with mascarpone, one tiramisu between two – it tastes all the better eaten together!

Condensed milk on a slice of bread

Serves 1
Preparation time: 3 minutes

¼ fresh baguette
sweetened condensed milk

Cut the baguette in half lengthways. Remove the soft crumb and cover the bread with a layer of condensed milk. It's up to you how thickly you spread it on the baguette!

Slice of bread with 'milk jam'

Serves 1 slice
Preparation time: 1 minute

1 slice of pain de campagne (or French bread), cut quite thick
1 pot of 'milk jam' (see recipe on page 18)

Spread the slice of bread with a generous layer of 'milk jam'. Bliss!

Coconut drops

Serves 4
Preparation time: 5 minutes
Chilling time: 15 minutes

125 g (4 oz) grated coconut
4 tablespoons sweetened condensed milk

Put the grated coconut and condensed milk into a large bowl. Mix with a spoon then shape into small balls, about the size of large marbles.
Put them into the freezer for 15 minutes. Roll them quickly in the remainder of the grated coconut. Eat well chilled.

Coconut drops

Semolina with lemon

Semolina with soya milk

Semolina with lemon

Serves 2
Preparation time: 5 minutes
Cooking time: 10 minutes

grated rind of ½ unwaxed lemon
500 ml (17 fl oz) milk
75 g (3 oz) fine semolina
2 tablespoons ground almonds
3 tablespoons caster sugar

Finely grate the peel of the half-lemon.
Heat the milk in a heavy-based saucepan.
As soon as it begins to simmer, pour in the
semolina, while stirring continuously with a
wooden spoon. Stir in the ground almonds
and grated lemon rind, and allow to cook
for about 8 minutes. Stir regularly to avoid
the semolina sticking to the bottom of the
saucepan and to prevent lumps forming.
Remove the saucepan from the heat, add
the caster sugar, stir well and pour into two
small dishes.
Serve lukewarm or cold.

Semolina with soya milk

Serves 2
Preparation time: 5 minutes
Cooking time: 10 minutes

500 ml (17 fl oz) soya milk
75 g (3 oz) fine semolina
2 teaspoons vanilla essence
caster sugar to taste

Heat the soya milk in a heavy-based saucepan.
As soon as it starts to simmer, pour in the
semolina, while stirring continuously with
a wooden spoon. Allow to cook for about
8 minutes.
Stir regularly to avoid the semolina sticking to
the bottom of the saucepan and to prevent
lumps forming.
Remove the saucepan from the heat and stir
in the vanilla essence and caster sugar to taste.
Pour into small bowls.
You can enjoy this lukewarm or cold.

Vanilla-flavoured tapioca

Serves 1–2 people
Preparation time: 5 minutes
Cooking time: 5 minutes

400 ml (14 fl oz) milk
2 tablespoons tapioca
½ teaspoon vanilla essence
1 tablespoon caster sugar

Bring the milk to the boil in a heavy-based
saucepan. Pour in the tapioca while stirring
continuously with a wooden spoon. Let it
cook for about 4 minutes over a low heat.
Stir in the vanilla essence and caster sugar.
Pour into a bowl and leave until lukewarm.
Eat lukewarm or cold.

Tapioca with coconut

Serves 1–2 people
Preparation time: 5 minutes
Cooking time: 5 minutes

400 ml (14 fl oz) milk
2 tablespoons tapioca
2 tablespoons Demerara sugar
2 tablespoons grated coconut

Bring the milk to the boil in a heavy-based
saucepan. Pour in the tapioca while stirring
continuously with a wooden spoon. Let it
cook for about 4 minutes over a low heat.
Stir in the sugar and grated coconut. Pour
into a bowl and leave until lukewarm.

Vanilla-flavoured tapioca

White risotto

Serves 2
Preparation time: 5 minutes
Cooking time: 25 minutes

25 g (1 oz) unsalted butter
100 g (3½ oz) risotto rice (arborio, carnaroli)
3½ tablespoons white wine
250 ml (8 fl oz) chicken stock
250 ml (8 fl oz) coconut milk
12 small cooked prawns
2 stalks lemon grass, white part only,
thinly sliced
½ grapefruit, segments removed and
cut into pieces
freshly ground salt and pepper
2 tablespoons grated Parmesan cheese

Melt half the butter in a heavy-based saucepan
and add the rice. Stir to coat all the grains with
the butter for a few moments and add the white
wine. Leave the rice to absorb this before pouring
in a little of the chicken stock, then wait for the
rice to absorb this liquid before adding another
3 or 4 tablespoons of stock. Continue to add the
stock and coconut milk in stages until both are
used up. Cover and let the rice cook over a very
low heat, checking from time to time that it isn't
sticking to the saucepan.
Quickly rinse and drain the prawns. Melt the
remaining butter in a non-stick frying pan and
put in the lemon grass and grapefruit pieces.
Let them fry for a couple of minutes then add
the prawns and cook over a very low heat for
2 or 3 minutes longer.
Add the prawns and grapefruit to your risotto.
Season, and mix in the grated Parmesan. Serve
as soon as the risotto is nice and creamy.

Monkfish with Parmesan cheese shavings

Serves 2
Preparation time: 10 minutes
Cooking time: 25 minutes

2 slices monkfish tail
50 g (2 oz) Parmesan cheese shavings

For the court-bouillon:
500 ml (17 fl oz) water
150 ml (¼ pint) dry white wine
1 small bouquet garni (sprig each of
parsley and thyme, bay leaf)
1 lemon slice
fine salt
pinch of allspice

Put the water in a saucepan, add the white wine, bouquet garni and lemon slice and heat gently. Leave to simmer, covered, for 15 minutes. Meanwhile, preheat the grill.
Add the slices of monkfish to the court-bouillon and let them poach for about 5 minutes. Remove the monkfish slices with a slotted spoon and drain them carefully. Put a few grains of fine salt and a touch of ground allspice on each slice.
Arrange the slices in a heatproof dish. Sprinkle over the Parmesan shavings. Pop the monkfish under the grill for 1 minute and serve immediately.

Scallops with saffron

Serves 2
Preparation time: 5 minutes
Cooking time: 12 minutes

100 ml (3½ fl oz) crème fraîche
100 g (3½ oz) creamy Greek-style yogurt
3 saffron strands
olive oil
6 scallops
butter

Gently heat the crème fraîche and the yogurt
together in a heavy-based saucepan. Put in
the strands of saffron. As soon as it begins
to simmer, remove from the heat, cover and
leave to infuse for about 5 minutes.
Heat a little olive oil in a non-stick pan. Season
the scallops very lightly and place them in the
smoking oil. As soon as they begin to brown,
turn them over and add a knob of butter.
Let them colour slightly, basting with the sauce.
After they have cooked for about 5 minutes,
drain and keep warm.
Serve the scallops on a bed of the saffron sauce.

Cheesecake on a ginger biscuit base

Panacotta

Cheesecake on a ginger biscuit base

Preparation time: 15 minutes
Cooking time: 35 minutes
Cooling time: about 1 hour
Chilling time: 1 hour

1 round deep tin about 23 cm (9 inches) in diameter, a springform tin is best as this makes it easier to remove the cheesecake

200 g (7 oz) ginger biscuits
60 g (2½ oz) butter, cut into pieces, plus extra for greasing
600 g (1¼ lb) fromage blanc
200 ml (7 fl oz) thick crème fraîche
caster sugar
1 teaspoon vanilla essence
pinch of cinnamon
pinch of salt
3 eggs
1 tablespoon maple syrup

Preheat the oven to 150°C (300°F) Gas Mark 2. Grease the sides and base of the cake tin with butter.
Crush the biscuits in the bowl of a food processor, or with a rolling pin, and pour the crumbs into a large mixing bowl. Put the pieces of butter into a small heavy-based saucepan over low heat until melted. Pour the melted butter over the biscuit crumbs and mix well.
Put the biscuit-crumb mixture on the base of the tin and and press it down with the palm of your hand to make a firm, even layer.
Pour the fromage blanc and crème fraîche into a large bowl and whisk. Add the caster sugar, vanilla essence, and a pinch each of ground cinnamon and salt, whisking all the time.
Add the eggs one by one and the tablespoon of maple syrup while mixing continuously.
Pour the mixture into the tin and bake for about 35 minutes.
Once out of the oven, wait for 5 minutes before loosening the edges with a knife. Leave to cool for another 5 minutes, before turning out to cool completely. Place in the refrigerator for 1 hour before serving.

Panacotta

Serves 4
Preparation time: 10 minutes
Cooking time: 5 minutes
Cooling time: 3 hours

2 gelatine leaves
250 ml (8 fl oz) milk
250 ml (8 fl oz) whipping cream
1 vanilla pod
75 g (3 oz) caster sugar

Separate the gelatine leaves and put them in a bowl of cold water. Pour the milk into a heavy-based saucepan and stir in the whipping cream. Cut the vanilla pod in two lengthways and scrape out the seeds Add the seeds and vanilla pod to the milk and cream mixture. Add the sugar and stir. Bring to a simmer then remove from the heat.
Cover and leave to infuse for 5 minutes.
Take out the vanilla pod. Squeeze any excess water from the gelatine leaves and put them into the warm creamy milk, stirring until they melt. Pour into glasses, or a mould, and stand in a cool place, or refrigerator, for 3 hours.

Vaporetto mousse with mascarpone

Serves 2
Preparation time: 5 minutes

200 g (7 oz) mascarpone
1 tablespoon acacia honey
4–5 cardamom pods
100 ml (3½ fl oz) whipping cream, chilled

Pour the mascarpone and honey into a large bowl and whisk rapidly.
Open the cardamom pods and carefully empty out the seeds. Grind them to a powder in a pestle or mortar, but if you have a spice grinder your task will be easier. Pour the well-chilled whipping cream into a large bowl, add a pinch of the ground cardamom seeds, or more to taste, and whip it with an electric whisk until it is light and airy.
Fold the whipped cream and mascarpone together.
Put the vaporetto mousse into 2 small bowls and serve well chilled.

Vaporetto mousse with mascarpone

Souvenir of Brazil

Rice pudding Venetian-style

Souvenir of Brazil

Serves 2
Preparation time: 10 minutes
Cooking time: 3 minutes
Chilling time: 1 hour

2 small clear glass individual moulds

100 ml (3½ fl oz) water
2 gelatine leaves
200 ml (7 fl oz) sweetened condensed milk
100 ml (3½ fl oz) papaya juice
100 ml (3½ fl oz) passion fruit juice

Pour the water into a saucepan and add the gelatine leaves. Let them soften for 5–10 minutes then put the saucepan over medium heat and bring to the boil. Remove from the heat, cover, and leave the gelatine to dissolve.
Quickly whip the condensed milk and the two fruit juices together with a whisk and mix into the dissolved gelatine. Pour the mixture into the moulds and place them in the refrigerator until the mousse is quite firm.
Eat well chilled with a few exotic fruits.

Rice pudding Venetian-style

Serves 2
Preparation time: 5 minutes
Cooking time: 1 hour

75 g (3 oz) pudding rice
500 ml (17 fl oz) milk
3 saffron strands
50 g (2 oz) caster sugar
2 tablespoons flaked almonds
20 g (¾ oz) unsalted butter

Rinse the rice quickly and drain. Fill a saucepan with water, bring it to the boil. Add the rice and leave it to simmer for 3–5 minutes. Drain and set aside.
Pour the milk into a large heavy-based saucepan and add the saffron. Bring to the boil and add the rice. Cover the pan and allow it to cook over a very low heat for about 45 minutes. Stir from time to time to stop it sticking to the bottom. Add the caster sugar and almonds, mix them in quickly, add the butter, cover and leave to cook for 2–3 minutes longer over a low heat.
Spoon the rice pudding into the serving bowls, remove the saffron and leave to cool. Put in a refrigerator and serve ice cold, unless you prefer to eat it lukewarm.

Sweet couscous with milk and dried fruit

Serves 2
Preparation time: 5 minutes
Cooking time: 5 minutes

5 dates
150 ml (¼ pint) milk
pinch of salt
pinch of ground cinnamon
bowl of fine, pre-cooked couscous, quantity to suit appetites
knob of butter
25 g (2 oz) blanched almonds
25 g (2 oz) raisins

Cut the dates in half lengthways, take out the stones, then cut the dates into strips.
Heat the milk in a small heavy-based saucepan. Remove from the heat and add the pinch of salt and ground cinnamon, together with the couscous. Stir and leave it covered for 3 minutes to swell.
Add the knob of butter, dates, almonds and raisins. Heat over a very low light for 3–4 minutes, separating the grains of couscous with a fork. Serve immediately with a glass of milk or tea.

Sweet couscous with milk and dried fruit

Catalan cream

For 2–4 people
Preparation time: 5 minutes
Cooking time: 12 minutes

750 ml (1¼ pints) milk
Grated rind of 1 unwaxed lemon
½ cinnamon stick
6 eggs
1 tablespoon cornflour
175 g (6 oz) caster sugar

Pour 500 ml (17 fl oz) of the milk into a saucepan. Add the grated lemon rind and the cinnamon. Bring to the boil and remove from the heat straight away. Cover and leave to infuse.
Break the eggs into a large bowl and whisk quickly.
Mix the cornflour into the remainder of the milk and add the mixture to the eggs in the bowl. Whisk and fold in the caster sugar.
Replace the saucepan of milk over a low heat and gradually pour the contents of the bowl into the saucepan, stirring continuously.
When the cream has thickened, remove the cinnamon stick. Pour into small heat-resistant moulds, leave to cool, then store in the refrigerator.
When you are ready to serve, you can sprinkle a tablespoon of sugar over each of the creams and pop them under a very hot grill until the sugar melts and caramelizes.

'One for two' tiramisu

Serves 2
Preparation time: 15 minutes
Chilling time: 6 hours

1 gratin dish, about 26 cm (10 inches) long

3 very fresh eggs, separated
50 g (2 oz) caster sugar
1 teaspoon vanilla essence
pinch of salt
300 g (10 oz) mascarpone
300 ml (½ pint) coffee
2 tablespoons rum
40 sponge fingers
cocoa powder

Put the egg yolks into a large bowl. Add the caster sugar and vanilla essence and whisk until the mixture becomes pale.
Put the egg whites into another large bowl, add a small pinch of salt, and whisk them until they stand up in peaks.
Spoon the mascarpone into a bowl and whisk lightly with a fork to incorporate some air. Gradually fold the whisked mascarpone into the egg and sugar mixture. Gently fold in the egg whites.
Pour the coffee and rum into a shallow bowl and quickly dip in half the sponge fingers. Arrange them in the bottom of the gratin dish then cover them with a layer of half the mascarpone cream. Dip the rest of the sponge fingers into the coffee and arrange them on top of the mascarpone cream in a single layer. Finally, top the sponge fingers with the remaining mascarpone cream.
Cover with clingfilm and place in the refrigerator for about 6 hours. Serve well chilled.
When you are ready to serve, sift a little cocoa powder over the top using a small sieve.

irresistible desserts

Those fatal weaknesses: wonderfully mouth-watering, delicious confections such as Chantilly and Fontainebleau – desserts made for kings.
They offer a sense of indulgence, extravagance, luxury and pleasure. What bliss! They brightened up the lives of kings and now ours too!

Mont Blanc

Frosted cup

Serves 2
Preparation time: 10 minutes

1 cocktail shaker or mixer
2 tall narrow glasses

2 scoops lime sorbet
2 scoops pineapple sorbet
2 scoops ginger sorbet
crushed ice
1½ tablespoons lime juice
75 ml (3 fl oz) vodka
3 tablespoons pineapple juice

Put 1 scoop of each sorbet into each glass.
Put the crushed ice into the shaker. Add the
lime juice, vodka and pineapple juice and shake
vigorously.
Fill the glasses and serve immediately.

Mont Blanc

Serves 4
Preparation time: 10 minutes

4 glasses on stems

8–12 small plain meringues
250 ml (8 fl oz) whipping cream, chilled
2 tablespoons icing sugar
400 g (13 oz) sweet vanilla-flavoured
chestnut purée

Crumble the meringues and divide them between
the glasses.
Put the chilled whipping cream into a large bowl
and whip with an electric whisk, until it can form
soft peaks but is not stiff. Add the icing sugar and
whisk lightly to incorporate. Cover the layer of
meringue with chestnut purée and then make
little domes of whipped cream (Chantilly cream).
Serve immediately.

Vanilla soufflé

Serves 4
Preparation time: 25 minutes
Cooking time: 40 minutes

1 soufflé dish, about 20 cm (8 inch) in diameter

knob of butter
100 g (3½ oz) caster sugar
250 ml (8 fl oz) milk
2 eggs
2 tablespoons cornflour
1 teaspoon vanilla essence
4 egg whites
pinch of salt
icing sugar

Preheat the oven to 180°C (350°F) Gas Mark 4.
Butter the soufflé dish and dust the sides with
caster sugar.
Pour the milk into a saucepan and heat gently.
Break the 2 eggs into a large bowl, add 75 g
(3 oz) caster sugar and mix well, then stir in the
cornflour and vanilla essence. Pour the hot milk
into the mixture, stirring continuously.
Pour the custard back into the saucepan and
cook over a low heat, stirring all the time.
When the mixture has thickened, remove from
the heat and leave it to cool.
Put the egg whites into a large bowl, add the
pinch of salt and beat them with an electric
whisk until they stand up in stiff peaks. Add
the remaining caster sugar and whisk again.
Gradually fold the beaten egg whites into the
custard using a spatula. Fill the prepared soufflé
dish with the mixture and place in the preheated
oven for about 30 minutes. Sift icing sugar over
the top and serve warm.

Apricot and mango cocktail with milk meringue

Fontainebleau à la Chantilly

Serves 4
Preparation time: 10 minutes
Chilling time: overnight

4 small pots, or ramekins
4 pieces of muslin to line pots

300 ml (½ pint) whipping cream, well chilled
30 g (1¼ oz) icing sugar
350 g (12 oz) smooth fromage blanc,
40% fat content

For the crème Chantilly:
150 ml (¼ pint) whipping cream, well chilled
30 g (1¼ oz) icing sugar

To make the Fontainebleau, pour the whipping cream into a large bowl, add the icing sugar and whisk until it forms soft peaks, then gradually fold in the fromage blanc.
Put a square of muslin into each mould. Fill it with the creamy mixture, fold the muslin over on top and store in a cool place, or refrigerator, overnight.
To make the crème Chantilly, pour the well-chilled whipping cream into a large bowl and whisk with an electric whisk. When it can make soft peaks, add the icing sugar, mixing it in with a spatula. Serve the Fontainebleau with as much crème Chantilly as desired.

Tip: The muslin is recommended but not essential.

Apricot and mango cocktail with milk meringue

Serves 2–4 people
Preparation time: 5 minutes

4 very ripe apricots
1 mango
250 ml (8 fl oz) milk
1 large meringue

Wash and dry the apricots, cut them in half and remove the stones. Peel the mango and cut the flesh into pieces. Put the fruit into a liquidizer and blend until you have a thick pulp. Pour into tall glasses.
Clean the bowl of the liquidizer and pour in the milk. Crumble the meringue and add to the milk and briefly blend together.
Pour the milk meringue over the fruit cocktail. Serve chilled.

Sautéed apples with hot milk and honey

Serves 2
Preparation time: 10 minutes
Cooking time: 15 minutes

3 nice apples (Cox' orange pippins, Braeburn …)
knob of butter
pinch of ground cinnamon
200 ml (7 fl oz) milk
2 tablespoons flower honey

Peel the apples, cut them into quarters and take out the cores and pips. Cut them into fairly thick slices.
Melt the butter in a frying pan and put the apple slices in to brown gently for about 15 minutes. They should be soft all the way through.
Sprinkle over a pinch of cinnamon.
In a small saucepan, heat the milk and honey over a low heat.
Put the sautéed apples into 2 bowls, cover with the hot milk and honey and serve.

Exotic fruits with whipped cream

Exotic fruits with whipped cream

Serves 4
Preparation time: 30 minutes
Chilling time: 20 minutes

4 tall clear glasses

4 bananas
4 passion fruits
4 kiwi fruit
250 ml (8 fl oz) whipping cream
50 g (2 oz) icing sugar

Cut the bananas into slices. Cut the passion fruits in two and scoop out the pulp. Put the bananas and passion fruit pulp into a liquidizer bowl and blend until it is smooth. Put into a bowl and place in the refrigerator for 20 minutes. Rinse out the liquidizer bowl.
Peel the kiwi fruit, cut them into slices and blend in the liquidizer until you have a smooth mixture.
Put the well-chilled whipping cream into a large bowl and whip rapidly with an electric whisk. Pour in the icing sugar as soon as the cream has increased in volume. Pour the kiwi purée into the glasses, spoon in a layer of the whipped cream and top with the banana and passion fruit purée.
Serve well chilled.

Iced banana

Serves 2
Preparation time: 5 minutes

1 banana
2 scoops of vanilla ice cream
125 ml (4 fl oz) chilled milk
1 tablespoon rum

Cut the banana into slices and place in the bowl of a liquidizer together with the ice cream, milk and rum. Blend them all together and pour into 2 glasses.

Milk soup

Serves 4
Preparation time: 5 minutes
Cooking time: 15 minutes

1 onion
1 canned celery heart
knob of butter
oil
500 ml (17 fl oz) milk
1 tablespoon honey
freshly ground pepper
2 pinches of salt

Peel the onion and rinse and drain the celery heart. Chop these two ingredients very finely. Melt a knob of butter in a casserole dish over medium heat and add a little oil. When hot, put in the chopped onion and celery heart. Turn down the heat and leave to cook gently for about 8 minutes. Pour in the milk and honey and cover the casserole. Let it simmer for 10–12 minutes. Add a generous amount of pepper together with some salt and serve very hot with a slice of toasted pain de campagne or French bread.

Vanilla brose

Serves 2
Preparation time: 5 minutes
Cooking time: 2 minutes

300 ml (½ pint) thin porridge (made using 1 cup porridge oats to 2 cups water or milk and water)
1 tablespoon Demerara sugar
½ teaspoon vanilla essence

Make the porridge in a saucepan by mixing together the oats, milk and water and heating until the mixture thickens slightly, stirring continuously. Then add the Demerara sugar and vanilla essence. Pour the liquid into 2 glasses and leave until lukewarm.

Hot soya milk

Serves 2
Preparation time: 5 minutes
Cooking time: 2 minutes

300 ml (½ pint) soya milk
1 tablespoon Demerara sugar

Gently heat the soya milk and Demerara sugar in a saucepan.
Pour into 2 tall glasses and serve lukewarm.

Coconut milk

Serves 4
Preparation time: 25 minutes

1 fresh coconut

Preheat the oven to 120°C (250°F) Gas Mark 1/2. Break the coconut in half, place the halves on a baking sheet, and bake for about 15 minutes. Separate the coconut from its shell with the point of a knife. Remove the thin brown skin then chop the coconut into small pieces. Divide the coconut pieces into 2 equal portions. Place one portion and 500 ml (17 fl oz) of cold water in a liquidizer and blend until smooth. Then put the liquid through a fine sieve. Put the second portion of coconut pieces into the liquidizer, add 500 ml (17 fl oz) of water, and repeat the process. Serve chilled.

rice cream pots with coconut

Little cream pots with coconut

Serves 6–8
Preparation time: 10 minutes
Cooking time: 15 minutes
Chilling time: overnight

6–8 small heatproof ramekins
roasting tin for the bain-marie

400 ml (14 fl oz) unsweetened condensed milk
1 litre (1¾ pints) milk
4 eggs
125 g (4 oz) grated coconut
125 g (4 oz) caster sugar
1 taspoon vanilla essence

Preheat the oven to 180°C (350°F) Gas Mark 4.
Put a kettle of water on to boil.
Pour the milk into a large bowl, add the
condensed milk and eggs. Whisk thoroughly
to blend. Add the grated coconut, caster sugar
and vanilla essence. Mix well then pour into the
ramekins. Put the ramekins in the roasting tin,
place it on the oven shelf, and slide the shelf
out sufficiently for you to pour in the simmering
water to two-thirds up the sides of the ramekins.
Slide the shelf carefully back into the oven and
bake for about 12–15 minutes. Check that they
are cooked then leave to cool.
Cover the ramekins with clingfilm and place in
the refrigerator overnight.
Serve well chilled.

Upside down petits-suisses

Serves 1
Preparation time: 5 minutes

2 petits-suisses
2 tablespoons milk
1 tablespoon Demerara sugar

Remove the petits-suisses from the refrigerator at
the last minute. Turn them out into a small bowl,
pour over the milk and top with Demerara sugar.

Condensed milk in a small spoon

Serves 1
Preparation time: 1 minute

1 small spoon

condensed milk

If you can find condensed milk packed in a tube,
then just unscrew the cap and pour it straight
into the spoon and eat. However, if you are a
fan of condensed milk, you will have a whole
can in the refrigerator – all ready for you to dip
into. Remove the condensed milk in advance
from the refrigerator and let it reach room
temperature. If you prefer things icy cold however,
leave it in the refrigerator or put it in the freezer
for a few minutes.

Yogurt ice cream

Serves 4
Preparation time: 10 minutes
Freezing time: several hours depending
on the freezer

An ice cream maker or metal tray

250 ml (8 fl oz) water
100 g (3½ oz) caster sugar
100 ml (3½ fl oz) double cream
450 g (¾ pint) Greek-style creamy yogurts
4 tablespoons lemon juice

Pour the water into a saucepan and place over
gentle heat. Add the sugar and when it has
completely dissolved, remove from the heat
and leave until lukewarm.
Mix together the double cream, yogurt and
lemon juice, then add the sugar syrup and
mix again.
Pour the mixture into the ice cream maker.
If you do not have an ice cream maker, you can
use a metal tray or plastic box and put it straight
in the freezer. If you do this you will need to mix
it up with a fork at regular intervals to break up
the ice crystals, until the mixture takes on the
consistency of ice cream.

Marquise blanche

Serves 2–4

Some tall thin glasses, like champagne flutes

About 10 tablespoons vanilla ice cream
1 large plain meringue

Remove the vanilla ice cream from the refrigerator
about ten minutes before starting the recipe.
Crush the meringue into fine pieces.
Arrange a layer of meringue in the bottom of the
glasses. Then put a layer of vanilla ice cream on
top, pressing lightly to make sure the two layers
are packed tightly together. Continue alternating
the layers of meringue and vanilla ice cream until
you reach the top of the glasses.
Serve when the ice cream is beginning to melt.

Note: This recipe conjures up those white ladies,
or 'marquises blanches', who haunted the
French countryside in olden days, ghostly
symbols of pleasure and indulgence.

Milk liqueur

Makes 1 litre (1¾ pints)
Preparation time: 10 minutes
Standing time: 2 weeks

1 unwaxed lemon
500 ml (17 fl oz) milk
500 ml (17 fl oz) brandy
1 vanilla pod
caster sugar

Wash the lemon and cut it into slices.
Pour the milk and brandy into a decanter
then add the lemon slices and vanilla pod.
Leave to stand for about 2 weeks in a cool
place. Stir the liqueur daily.
When 2 weeks have elapsed, strain it through
a sieve. Add 2 tablespoons of caster sugar and
serve chilled.

indexes

recipes by chapter

Shops and Stockists of Tableware:

Astier de Villatte: 173 rue Saint Honoré 75001 Paris
Azag: 9 rue François Miron 75004 Paris
Bodum: www.bodum.com
Chône: 60 rue Vieille du Temple 75003 Paris
Cuisinophilie: 28 rue du Bourg Tibourg 75004 Paris
Happy home: 76 rue François Miron 75004 Paris
Home Autour du Monde: 8 rue des Francs Bourgeois 75004 Paris
Ikea: www.ikea.fr
Kitchen Bazaar: 23, bd de la Madeleine 75001 Paris
La forge subtile: 3 rue Henry de Jouvenel 75006 Paris
La Samaritaine: www.lasamaritaine.com
Maison de famille: 29 rue Saint Sulpice 75006 Paris
Muji: www.muji.co.uk
Résonances: www.resonances.fr
Tsé-Tsé at Galerie Sentou 24 rue du Pont Louis-Philippe 75004 Paris

Acknowledgements
Thanks to Magali Harivel and Gabriella Berglund
Special thanks to Laurence for her role in creating the mood and flavour of this book.

First published by Marabout, an imprint of Hachette Livre
43 Quai de Grenelle, Paris 75905, Cedex 15, France
Under the title *Délices de Lait*
© 2003, Marabout (Hachette Livre)
All rights reserved

English language translation produced by Translate-A-Book, Oxford

This edition published by Hachette Illustrated UK, Octopus Publishing Group Ltd.,
2–4 Heron Quays, London, E14 4JP
English Translation © 2004, Octopus Publishing Group Ltd, London

Text: Laurence and Gilles Laurendon. Testing of recipes: Ilona Chovancova.
Shopping: Stéphanie Bey.
Photographs © Akiko Ida, © Pierre Javelle.
Proofreading and corrections (French edition): Antoine Pinchot and Véronique Dussidour

ISBN: 1-84430-094-3
Printed by Tien Wah Press, Singapore